Getting Past Your Breakup

Your Relationship Ended but Your Life Didn't

Shelby Grant

ISBN-13:
978-0615951829 (WOS Publishing)

ISBN-10:
0615951821

WOS Publishing: First Printing, 2014

Printed in the United States of America

Table of Contents

Introduction

"It's over."
"We need to talk."
"It's not you, it's me."
"I think we need to take a break."
"I love you, but I'm not in love with you."

Let's face it. There is no nice way to end a relationship. Every time a relationship ends, pieces of you have been taken away and all that is left is a hole. In that hole lies emotions that feel like they will swallow you whole and you will lose yourself completely. You may find that you're becoming a bit of a recluse and you just don't want to get out of bed. Who wants to get out of bed and face the world, when the person who was an integral part of your life is no longer there?

I was one of those people who believed that my life had ended when my first love broke up with me. We shared an apartment together. We worked together. We were together practically 24/7. He broke up with me a few days before Valentine's Day.

What was his reasoning? He said that he didn't feel that same spark as when we first started dating. I was devastated. I felt like my world was falling apart. I cried and cried. The moving on process was so difficult because we still lived together and we still worked together. We were still having sex. We had talks about getting back together. There were even mentions of marriage.

This went on for a few months. Things were picking up and we were getting along better. I was hopeful.

April came around and it was time to renew the lease on the apartment we shared. We talked and I was still under the impression that we would continue to work on our relationship and work toward getting back together.
I signed the lease. He signed the lease.
I was hopeful. He turned into a dick.

He began to use drugs more. He would be mean and say things to his friends about me when I was in the room. He was doing everything he could to hurt me. He no longer wanted to go on walks with me. He started sleeping on the couch, and would only come to bed to have sex. He moved his stuff out of the bedroom and fashioned a room out of the dining room. He hung a sheet for privacy.

I began to grow bitter and angry. We got into more arguments and that's when I learned the truth. Even though he agreed with me, he hated me for aborting our baby. He pretended to want to get back together because his credit was horrible and he nowhere else to go—whereas I could easily walk away from the apartment because I could go back to my parents. He used me. We didn't speak for a few days after that fight. We slowly grew to become civil toward one another again; we did share an apartment still.

One day he went too far. He came into my bed and tried to have sex with me. When I told him no, and went from my bed to his, just to get away from him, he followed and tried again. Again, I said no and went back to my own bed. I shut the door and he didn't come in for a little while.

When I started to fall back asleep, he came in and pulled my pants down and tried to rape me. After fighting him off, I got dressed and went to work. I didn't go back to the apartment that night; I stayed at my mom's house. I went back when I knew he wouldn't be there and packed the rest of my things and officially moved out.

The reason I shared my story with you was partially for me and partially for you. After that traumatic break up, I didn't know how to feel normal again. I felt like I was flawed and that I was worthless. I couldn't wrap my head around the knowledge that someone I had loved so deeply could hurt me in such a demeaning and intrusive way.

The healing process from that break up was a hard one. There were times where I wanted to give up. There were times where I wanted to go to him and bash his face in. There were times that I was numb. Hell, even on a few rare occasions, there were times where I was actually happy. As time went on, the rage and bitterness subsided and the contentment and even happiness came more frequently. I didn't have a method to my healing. I often followed the "fake it 'til you make it" mantra. Looking back, I don't think that was entirely effective. There are still some moments where the resentment toward him bubbles to the surface. And as much as I don't want to admit, there are times that I miss him too. This particular relationship ended seven years ago, so as you can tell, it's still a work in progress.

The point of this book is to help those who are going through a break up and feel like things are falling apart. It is my hope that by reading this, you will be able to begin the healing process. It is my hope that you won't be like me and succumb to those moments of nostalgia and let them take over.

I don't want to think of this book as a self-help book. I believe that mending your heart after a break up is more than self-help. It's about healing your heart and your soul. It's about realizing that it is okay to cry and mourn over the good memories that your relationship gave you. It is my hope that the contents within these pages can offer you some solace, even if it is brief.

I'll Cry If I Want To

It's Okay to Mourn Your Relationship

His side of the closet is empty, tooth brush is missing, and his key has been sitting on the table for a few days now. If you look around, you have flash backs to moments that you two shared in the apartment. You may feel like you can't live there anymore because every room and every piece of furniture has some memory linked to it. The knot in your stomach and the lump in your throat keep coming back. You steel yourself, refusing yourself to let the tears flow...

I remember my first night sleeping alone. I couldn't get comfortable, the silence bothered me, and I just couldn't stop crying—I cried a lot; and I hated myself for it. I felt like I was letting him win. I felt like I was weak because I was mourning a relationship that turned so toxic. In a way, I felt like I was reaffirming every negative he had said about me.

Well you know what? He was wrong. I was nothing like the things he said about me. What's even more important, I was not weak for crying. I was not letting him win. After every cry, every break down, I felt a little bit better. I couldn't explain why it worked, but it did.

A break up is never easy to get over. Some people say, "Oh they were an asshole, you don't need to cry over them." Well you know what? They were your asshole. They meant something to you. They had qualities that made you fall in love with them. When people say insensitive things like you don't need to cry over them, don't listen to them, it's your heart that is broken, not theirs.

A broken heart may be a metaphor because your heart can't literally break. What isn't a metaphor is the heartache that you are feeling. Your emotions can and do cause pain. If you stub your toe or break your arm, your brain sends out pain signals. These are the very same signals that your brain sends out when you're experiencing emotional distress. To your brain, pain is pain, regardless the form.

We are social beings and we need interaction with other people. We form relationships and bonds with others. It is in these relationships and bonds that help us thrive. When we experience pain, be it physical or emotional, it is our body's way of saying something is wrong. The need for a social bond with another person is so strong; it is our instinct to do anything we can to prevent the pain from escalating further. Even though pain is our body's way of saying something is wrong and we recognize what is wrong, it doesn't make the pain go away.

Crying gives you a release from that pain. If you feel like you need to cry, go ahead and cry. Cry as hard as you need to. Sometimes you'll feel better and sometimes you won't; but don't let anyone tell you that you're being too emotional and that you need to stop. Your emotions shouldn't be ignored, and if you try to ignore them, you could end up feeling worse. If you just can't bring yourself to cry, reach out to someone and build a support system so that they can help you process your pain.

Support Systems

Even the Strongest Needs a Crutch Sometimes

It's been a few weeks since the break-up. You've managed to put on a brave face and the people in your life may think that you truly are okay.

You're able to go about your daily routine with some sort of normalcy. You make plans to go out with your friends and every time they ask how you are, you smile and give some sort of variant of, "I'm fine."

Inside, you're not. You feel your stomach turn in knots every time you say that false truth. Physically, you are fine. The pain is still inside though.

You've gotten better at hiding it. It's almost as though you are two different people. Alone, you are depressed and still mourning over the relationship that ended. When you're with other people, they see you as the person you used to be before the break-up.

During my grieving period, I refused to talk to anyone. I was that person who, even though my eyes are getting teary and my chin is quivering... I will not talk to you about what I'm feeling. This is probably one of my biggest flaws. If only I had talked to someone, I may have been able to move on with my life much sooner than I had. I had friends and family who were concerned about me. They would ask how I was and often times demand that I talk to them. Still, I didn't talk to them. Looking back, I wish I had. You know what they say; hind-sight is 20-20.

If there is one thing I've learned, it's to not bottle up my feelings. Those bottled up feelings will eat you up and spit you out; especially if you go over every word ever exchanged between the ex and yourself. When you wake up in the morning and you feel like it was the very first day alone after the break up, reach out to someone. You don't have to go about your day like nothing is wrong. You don't have to pretend that everything is okay.

Reach out to the people who care about you. Ask them to talk with you for a little while. If you don't want advice, just someone to listen, tell them that. Tell them that you aren't looking for anything more than support. Chances are the people you reach out to will be more than happy to listen to you. These people know you and they probably know the signs of when there is something you aren't telling them.

If you cannot talk to someone within your circle for whatever reason, there is the option of seeking the help of a professional. You may find that talking to a therapist or a counselor is easier than talking to someone you know. With a therapist, you essentially have a fresh ear to listen and offer advice. A fresh set of eyes, if you will. You may even find that you are talking about things that you weren't even aware of.

By talking to someone, you are not weak. Please, never think that you are not a strong because your emotions got the "best of you." People are social creatures. We need to maintain a connection with others, in good time and in bad. You may even find that every time you talk about your emotions and the heartache, that very ache may begin to subside. By the end of the conversation, you just may feel slightly better.

Journaling

I don't have to tell you how hard it is to get over someone, especially when that someone was someone you loved very much. From the second you can catch your breath again after hearing that it's over; your mind feels like it's in a tailspin. When you lay down to sleep, your mind doesn't want to rest. You find yourself staring into space just thinking about things. They could be insignificant things like the way you the way they would leave the cap off the toothpaste, to something as monumental as the first time you said 'I love you' to each other.

The tissues and the support group can only do so much for you. Sometimes you just need to be able to process your thoughts on your own. Sometimes, you just need to reflect on your past with that person without any outside perspective.

Journaling is a good way to do this. In journaling you can put your anger and grief down onto paper. You can reflect fondly on the good times and you can even write down your regrets.

I've filled up several journals and countless loose leaf pages after my break up. I wrote the whole spectrum; the good memories, the bad memories, reasons I was glad it was over, to reasons why it hurt so bad. During the days where I found myself missing him, I would reread a certain section and remember some of the bad times. It helped me realize that he wasn't as perfect as I may have thought he was. By reading the bad stuff helped me to remember that this break up ultimately is a good thing. When I felt that he was the Devil incarnate, I would read some of the happier times. It helped keep me from becoming too bitter and angry.

I realize that not everyone has had an exceptionally bad break up. I'm also aware that for some people, you may feel like everything is blissful and when the relationship ended, it came like a fist to the stomach. It may be harder for you to find the flaws in the relationship. Don't be mistaken though. You don't want to admit it, I know I didn't want to, but there are flaws in every relationship, either on your end or theirs. If it were all perfect, the relationship wouldn't have ended.

You may find that you can't bring yourself to read anything you've written. That's perfectly fine. You may want to burn the journals. That's fine also. These are your thoughts, memories, feelings. They are yours to do with as you wish.

16

Journaling and getting everything out can prove to be cathartic.

Just try it. You may find yourself staring at the paper, unsure of where to begin. Being faced with a blank sheet of paper and a mind constantly running, it can be overwhelming.

My suggestion would be to write the reason why you're staring at the paper. What made you pick up the journal at that particular moment? You may be surprised at what you end up writing.

Activity

Keep Busy Can Help Keep Your Mind off of the Pain

It's a simple thing, but being active can help you overcome some of the pain. People have said that working out helps. You know, especially the physical combat type workouts. Kick boxing, karate, using a punching bag—those sorts of things. What's the harm of little pseudo-fisticuffs? It's better than it being someone's face, that's all I'm saying.

All jokes aside, being active can help keep your mind off of things. It doesn't have to be anything crazy like pretending to punch someone's face in. You can go for walks, bike rides, go to the gym, or something as simple as yard work or just playing with your kids (if you have any, of course).

I must admit, I never got into the "being active" thing. I'm not much of an active person by nature. I did find that whenever I needed to clear my head and be alone, I would go for a walk. I'd take my MP3 player and just walk around the block a few times. Sometimes I would let a few tears fall, but most of the time I just felt a little calmer then before I left.

Your support system is a great way to help you get active. Grab a few friends and go play laser tag or go to the movies. Ask your friends if they would be willing to keep you doing things. You don't want to become a hermit, after all. You may want to plan a vacation with your closest friends. It will certainly get you out of the house and you'll have fun!

One thing I would suggest is to stay away from the activities that you and your ex used to do together; at least for a little while. I loved taking a ride on the ferry. Something about the rocking on the boat and it being so peaceful on the water made it that much more enjoyable. Well, I took my ex on the ferry and we would go on it several times each summer. After the break up, I couldn't go on the ferry for a few years. Finally, I decided it was time to let go and not let him take that away from me. I took my friends on the ferry and they loved it as much as I did. It took about 3 years.

Of course, it's all up to you if you want to forego the activity you and the ex shared together. It may or may not bring back some painful memories.

End Contact

Cutting the Ties that Bind

I have a confession. While I have been writing this, I've often thought about reaching out to an ex. I have moments of weakness sometimes and I've written a message to the ex. I never sent it though because I knew it would only cause me more pain. For the most part, I've done well with ending contact with the ex.

It's difficult to cut all contact in the beginning. You may find that sometimes you just want to hear their voice one more time. Don't give in and call. Now is the time to delete their phone number, unfriend them on Facebook, delete their email and IM. By deleting any contact information, you won't feel tempted to reach out. If they reach out to you, try your best to ignore their advances. Nothing good can come out of any conversation.

If you share mutual friends, ending contact can be difficult. Mutual friends will be aware of the break up, no doubt; however, there may be instances where parties are thrown and you may run into the ex. It'll be awkward, no doubt. Try not to let the run in phase you. If you're still hurting, try to put on a brave face and pay the ex no mind. If you run into your ex, keep it brief. Be cool and confident. This is where the phrase "fake it til you make it" can work, if even for only the evening.

Now, ending contact is easier for people who were only in a relationship, I realize this. Things get much more difficult if you have children.

Children are the innocent bystanders in a relationship that has ended. I needn't tell you how difficult the transition can be for them. When dealing with the other parent and the child is present, keep things cordial. There's no need to linger and make small talk though. Keep any interaction short and simple, only sharing the important information the other parent may need; this may include homework that needs to be done, illnesses or doctor's appointments, or discipline problems. One thing to always remember is to not talk poorly of the ex in front of the child. This probably sounds like a simple and common sense tip, but it can be difficult to keep negative words to yourself; especially if there are some bad feelings left; kids don't need to hear the problems you and your ex have.

Ending contact with an ex can be one of the harder aspects of getting over the relationship. It'll be hard for a while. You'll be tempted to see what they are doing on Facebook. You may have one too many drinks and want to spill your heart out to them. This is why it's a good idea to cut all contact and delete any contact information. It'll give you time to rethink the impulse to reach out.

Conclusion

A New Beginning without the Ex

A broken heart is something that everyone goes through at one point or another. No matter what the circumstances or the length of time a relationship lasts; when one ends it can be devastating. There is no sure fire way to get over someone. We all are different and we cope with things differently. What may work for me may not work for you. You may be the type of person who can get over things easily. Conversely, you may be the type of person who takes a long time to get over things. In that aspect, we are all unique.

I think that the main part of getting over a failed relationship is time. It's an over-used phrase but there is some truth behind it: "time heals all wounds". While the wound may leave a nasty scar, that scar is a reminder that you survived and you are stronger for it. How are you stronger? You now have a better idea of what you do and don't want in a future relationship. If you've been able to reflect on your past relationships objectively, you may see patterns that lead to the relationship ending. You know what to look for in the other person and what to spot in your own habits.

Giving yourself completely to someone else can be the cause of the best moments of your life and could bring the worst moments too. Allow some time for you. Pamper yourself, join a gym, and spend time with friends... Do things that will stimulate your mind and your well-being. Use this time to reflect and grow.

For myself, I'm still working on myself. I take steps to improve my outlook on life. My ex was a big part of my life for a few years. But because of him and that relationship, I now know that I deserve to be respected. I deserve to be treated like a person. I deserve to be happy. With the help of my friends and family I was able to get the love and comfort that I needed and when I needed it the most. Without those people, the healing process could have been much longer and that much harder.

I don't claim to have the answers on how to heal your heart. I won't say that the information in this book will help you. I certainly hope that it will though. I sincerely hope that you are able to finish this book and have a little clarity.

I guess what I'm saying is... Your relationship ended, not your life. Think of this as a chance for a new beginning.